# LETTERS FROM CATS

## Hilarious & Heartfelt Notes

*Letters from Cats: Hilarious and Heartfelt Notes*
Stacey Ritz.
Published by Rockville Publishing

Front cover photo: istockimages
Back cover photo: istockimages
Interior photos courtesy of Advocates 4 Animals/Stacey Ritz

ISBN: 978-1507651742

PRINTED IN THE UNITED STATES OF AMERICA

# Forward

I'VE OFTEN WONDERED what cats really think of humans. My foster turned forever cat, *Jazzi*, chases people around the house when she spots bare feet. She has a fetish for biting human toes. *One,* my special needs foster cat (yes, her name is really One), sees me enter the living room and quickly jumps onto the piano and scurries across the keys, always doting a unique tune. And then there's *Chewbacca.* The moment I enter the kitchen- day or night- she belts out a menacing meow and jumps up next to the sink, begging for a bowl of kitten milk; yet she is 11 years old. It's a long story…

Distinct quirks and a dash of pizzazz make each cat I meet different from the next. Cat lovers spend time musing about the hilarious behaviors and attitudes of felines. But what do the cats think? That's what I set out to explore in *Letters from Cats*. I wanted to hear directly from the cats themselves. When they bite our toes, is it simply for spite or do they have an ulterior motive? When they shred the toilet paper roll…again…is it a work of art or pure destruction? What, exactly, are they thinking? If you're curious, read on…

## -The Butler-

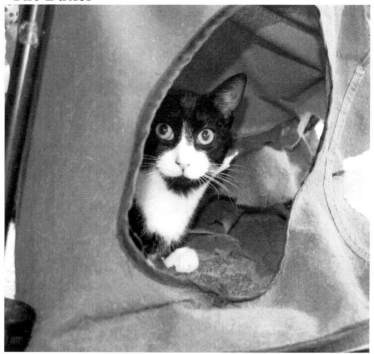

# Dear Guardian:

I knock your glasses off of the nightstand every morning at
3AM to alert you to your duties. I like to go outside to potty
at exactly 3AM. But you never seem to want to wake up. I
walk back and forth on your long hair a few times and
sometimes I will even walk across your face. You don't seem
to want to get up; but I know that you are proud to care for
me. *Why don't you want to get up?*

After I walk across your hair and face several times, I then
proceed to lie across your neck. Sometimes you will turn to
one side, but still, you never open your eyes! *I need to go
outside.*

Yes, I know I have a litter box. But I just like to go outside for a few minutes to do my business. Is it really too much to ask that you let me out, wait on me to potty and then let me back in? I know sometimes it is raining or snowing. I know that it is still dark outside. But I'm ready to go and I wish you were too.

After five or ten minutes of trying several calm tactics of waking you, you seem to leave me no choice. I know you are virtually blind without your glasses and I know you do not want them to break. Knowing this, I first spend some time pawing at your stomach – hoping maybe this will wake you. Generally it does not. Sometimes I fall off the side of the bed while trying to get your attention, but I don't let that stop me. I jump right back up and start all over again. I'm persistent.

But sometimes you leave me no choice. So I jump onto your nightstand and use my paw to knock the alarm clock onto the floor. This usually makes a big bang but it's still not enough. So then I knock your glasses onto the floor and just like magic- you're up!

Hurray! Hurray! You're sitting up and the next thing I know you're placing your feet on the ground to retrieve your glasses. But why are you always so grouchy in the mornings? You place your glasses on your eyes and pull a pair of warm socks over your feet and now I know we're finally on our way. I get to go outside- yippee!

You stumble slowly down the steps that lead to the back door as I skip along by your side. I rub your ankles and let out my loudest purr to thank you. But you never seem amused by my antics. And so I trot happily outside to do my business. I take in a breath of early morning air and watch as you wait at the window for me to return. But then I see a mouse- *a mouse*! Did you see it? And like lightening I'm off onto a new adventure. I know you're standing at the door waiting for me and I know when I return you'll curl into your cozy bed. Thank you for waiting on me. I'll just be a moment longer…

Oh, what's this? *Pounce…pounce.* I made a kill! I scoop it proudly into my mouth and run towards you to bring you a gift; showing you how much I love you. Only you do not want to let me in. I brought you a gift! I'm ready to return to the indoors now…ready to snuggle.

Love,
Rudy

**-Humans are so weird-**

# Dear people of this household:

I am a cat. Please do not expect me to be human. I do not expect you to be a cat.

You want me to learn tricks. I watch you do your own tricks - like clicking a button to answer the phone whenever it rings. I watch you run to the door each time it rings. If something buzzes or rings you rush to open it, answer it, or turn it off. But I am not impressed by *your* tricks.

You want me to follow rules. Cats don't do rules. We are independent creatures; free spirits and I don't intend on changing. My fellow cats would be ashamed if I even considered it! I like to jump on the kitchen counter when you are not looking. I like to push my new cat toys under the couch and piano, too. I eagerly wait for you to move the furniture so that I can have a large pile of toys again- only to push them all back under to the black abyss.

You want me to wear cute outfits. I do not need material things. I'll let you dress me up from time to time- for your amusement only. But I don't need fancy clothes. I am a cat.

You want me to watch television with you or read a book. I prefer to sit *on* your book- right on top of the page you are reading, so that you will instead pay attention to me. When you watch television, I prefer to jump on your shoulders, knead your hair, paw your lap and throw my toys around so that again, you will pay attention to *me* instead of to a talking screen.

You want me to go to bed and sleep through the night snuggled up close to you. But I nap most of the day and I prefer to sprint around the house when it's dark and run into random items, causing a bit of a stir. I enjoy sliding across the hardwood floors and meowing loudly with glee when I set a new record for how fast I can run in a circle to chase my tail.

After living in a human household for ten years, these are the things I have learned that human's do- and the things they wish that I did. But I am a cat and I always will be.
Cats are not humans. We like to squeeze ourselves in tiny boxes just for fun. *I've never seen a human do that!* You can buy us an expensive toy and we'll choose to play in the box it came in almost every time. You can buy us healthy food, but I'll always meow for the tastier (aka cheaper) stuff! We are cats. We do what we want, when we want.

What if cats wished that their humans were cats? It's something to think about.

Purrs,

Jazzi

## -We May Never Meet-

# Dear people who live here:

We haven't formerly met, but I wanted to write and thank
you for saving my life. You keep a heated water bowl out
during the bitterly cold winter months. You keep a full bowl
of dry cat food out too.

You saved my life.

Last year the people I called my guardians moved away and
put me outside to fend for myself. I have been lonely and
terrified since the day they left. I have also been heartbroken.
I loved them and tried to be the best cat I could be. I don't
know why they left me all alone. I had never been outdoors
before. Now I have taught myself to dodge the cars that race
up and down the street. I have learned how to keep warm by
hiding in bushes. I stay away from unaltered male cats- I do
not want to get pregnant, but it's hard out here. I also have to
keep my distance from wild animals like fox, coyotes and
raccoons.

When I eat and drink at your generous bowls I lift my face between each bite to make sure I won't be attacked from behind. One wrong move and I'll lose my life. Life is so different in the great outdoors.

I used to live indoors only and my former humans took my claws. I don't have any way to defend myself now except to use my smarts. I used to have a large pink bed; it was so soft and fluffy. Now I sleep in the coarse bushes that line the front of the houses in this neighborhood.

I've watched a new family move into my old home. I made a few appearances on the front porch, hoping that maybe they would take me in. Maybe I could be back inside of my old house again. But my efforts were to no avail. I am alone. But I have survived because of you. When the ground was frozen and cold, your supply of water saved me and it's saving me again today.

We may never meet. But you saved my life. A simple thank you doesn't seem to suffice. But thank you is all I have to offer right now.

Sincerely,

Stray cat

## -Wondering -

# Dear loyal guardians:

I have a question. It's one I've always wanted to ask. Where is my eye? Most cats have two. You have two eyes, too. But I only have one. Where did the other one go?

PS I've met others who have the same question...

Love,

peanlie

## -Oh Christmas Tree!-

# Dear Human Family:

Oh, what fun the holidays bring! I love sitting in the window and watching the snowflakes fall from the sky. I love the warmth that the fireplace brings during these cold winter months. I love the laughter and holiday cheer that typically fills the halls of this happy home. And I love the music that echo's off the walls- always upbeat and cheerful.

But what I love most about the holidays is that spectacular tree you place in the living room every year. While you humans pass around gifts, you give *me* a tree! Oh, you must really love me! You call it a Christmas tree, and I am honored you have named a tree after me. Yes, my name is

Chrissy- but Christmas is close enough! Oh the tree brings me so much delight. I try to contain myself but it's too much to ask. The twinkling lights, the dangling ornaments, the thick green branches that beg me to climb.

Once you tuck yourself into bed at night, I creep beneath the tree and one by one, I bat at the ornaments hanging from its bottom branches. I try. I really try. But the tree that you named after me is begging me to play. And who am I to argue?

When the ornaments fall to the ground, I chase them and toss them and occasionally collide into the wall while on this great adventure. I usually stop to bathe for a few minutes and I may even curl up under the Chrissy tree and take a short nap. But once I awake the tree is there again, begging me to play. I wake up surrounded by my bounty and proud as can be. It's still dark out and you are fast asleep. I still have hours to play!

I count the shiny objects that I've won and then I decide it's time to climb. I start out slowly at first. One branch at a time. I try to keep quiet but inevitably a few more ornaments fall to the ground, adding to my winnings. After I climb up the first few branches, I test out the limbs. I sit on one branch and then try another. Each branch gives me a new view of the house. Sometimes my head gets tangled in the twinkling lights but I don't mind. I just push right through. I climb higher and higher…and higher.

And once I reach the top, I find myself sitting side by side with a beautiful angel. I have done it! I've climbed the Chrissy tree! A few bright lights are twisted around my belly, but I have to take in this wonderful view. I can look down at the piano and the couch. I can touch the ceiling! In fact, I scratch it a few times as I bask in my glory. The angel doesn't have much to say and she won't pet me, so I begin my descent.

Climbing down the tree doesn't seem to go as smoothly as climbing up has gone. But I am not deterred.

I knock a few more ornaments off the tree and eagerly watch them fall to the ground. There are not many left on the tree now. I am twisted up in twinkle lights as I continue trying to climb down.

Oh, the sun is starting to come out. You'll be awake soon. I need to climb down- fast!

But I am twisted in the lights. I try to make progress to no avail. I am *really* twisted.

I find a cozy branch near the center of the Chrissy tree and curl up in a ball. This is as good of a spot as any to curl up for a nap. You won't know I'm here and I'll play again once you've left for work.

I drift quickly off to sleep but when I wake, I hear your voice. You are not happy. "Chrissy, you've destroyed the tree!" you shout. But I haven't destroyed anything. I've only been enjoying the toy you brought to me. This is my way of showing you how much I appreciate your efforts. I love the Chrissy tree!

I feel you carefully lift me from the tree and untangle me from the twinkling lights. I purr with delight, trying to thank you for such a fun gift. You place me on the floor and begin rehanging the ornaments and lights.

I'll nap for a while and when night comes, I'll have another night of fun in my tree. Oh Chrissy tree, Oh Chrissy tree how wonderful you are!

Purrs & Whiskers,

Chrissy

## -Just in Time-

# Dear Rescuer:

I wound up in a shelter behind bars. But I was innocent I tell you, innocent! I was merely trying my best to survive as a stray and someone didn't like me hanging around their yard and they took me away.

They placed me in a steel cage, no blanket to my name. A small bowl of food and water accompanied me but as hungry as I was, I could not eat. I don't know if the shelter workers knew my status, because they placed me on death row. I had one day left to live because no one wanted me around. But all I wanted to do was live. I didn't want to trouble anyone, but it seems that trouble is all anyone ever thought I was.

I was on death row, but it wasn't just me I was worried about. I had babies inside of me and they were ready to arrive. Didn't the shelter workers know?

I could hardly sleep that night in my lonely cage. I paced back and forth and prepared for my babies to arrive. They were coming. But the shelter workers said we were going-*tomorrow*. I didn't want to die. And I didn't want my babies to die either.

Sunlight came with the arrival of morning and I had never felt so sad in my entire life. I sat in my cramped cage and gave birth to three little ones. I bathed them and nursed them. I cuddled them close to me and tried to keep them warm. I did all of the things a good mother should do, even though I knew it would all be over soon.

When the shelter workers arrived they hardly gave a second glance to my newborn babies and me. I hoped they might forget we were here and maybe spare us an extra day of life.

But my heart sank when one worker solemnly came to my tiny steel cage and unlocked the latch. *Please don't let it happen*, I winced, begging for our lives. I purred and pawed, hoping to win him over. I pleaded with my eyes hoping that I could change his mind.

First, they took me away and placed me in a new cage. *My babies!* I cried- wanting my little ones by my side. *Please bring my babies to me!*

After a few moments my babies arrived and I snuggled them close for what I thought may be our last time.

It was hard to see through the crate walls, but from what I could tell we were placed in a vehicle and the motor turned on. *Oh no!* Where were we going? When would this end? Would my babies and I ever see daylight again?

I heard the frantic cries of other innocent felines in cages surrounding mine and wondered in a panic, what we all would endure.

A bit later I heard a friendly voice and pressed my gaunt eyes to the front of the crate, trying to get a look at what was taking place. Two kind ladies smiled as they looked back at me and then my crate was handed over to them and I knew instantly…

By some miracle I had been saved; my babies and me. We went to a place called *rescue* where we were able to breathe. We received proper vetting and then we were given a private room to ourselves. No more cages, no more fear. For the first time in my life, I was surrounded by someone who didn't long for me to be banished. I was wanted; I was free.

Thank you kind humans for saving our lives. It's been a year now and my babies have all been adopted, as have I. All of us are altered- no more babies to come. And now I'm sitting indoors basking in the rays of sun that pour through the windows.

Because of you, we are all alive and well. And because of you, we will never know harm again. Because of you, we know that kindness really does exist and because of you each of us have become part of a family- a family to call our very own.

Forever grateful,

Tia Maria

## -Panicked-

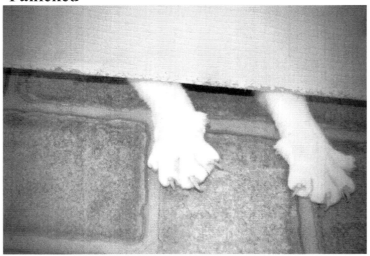

# Attention Humans:

Wait! Where did you go? I don't understand. I was just fast asleep on your lap and you got up and left again. You went into a tiny room and closed the door, even as I was chasing your feet. Why did you leave me? Have you been kidnapped?

I hear the sound of water flowing behind the door. You know I love to play in the sink! Why won't you let me in?

I desperately stick my paws under the door; first just one, then both front paws. I'm stressing out on the other side of this door. Can you see me? I'm here to save you! Someone closed you in the tiny room again and I just don't know why. Let me in! Let me in!

But you're not coming. I hear you in there. I start to meow and wave my paws beneath the door again and again. Maybe you'll see me! Maybe my paws will pull the door open so you can be set free. I miss you so much!

Oh wait- now I'm sure I hear water and I know it's a running sink. I have to get to you…

I am meowing as loud as I possibly can. I'm doing everything I can to get to you. Have you been kidnaped or did you leave me? You wouldn't leave me, I know you love me too much. *Right?*

My paws are waving frantically under the door. I hear more water.

Can you see me now?

Can you see me now?

Can you see me now?

Just when I am about ready to give up the door clicks and you reappear. I look behind you and I don't see a kidnapper anywhere. It's just you. You're here! You're safe! You're mine!

I look up towards you with my most loving eyes. *Follow me!* I trot eagerly to my food bowl and look at you again. Thank goodness you're okay!

Much Relieved,

Mr. Whiskers

## -Searching-

**Thank you.** I don't know your name and you don't know my past, but thank you.

To tell you the truth, I've been out here alone for years. Once upon a time, I had a home and I was happy. But it all abruptly ended one day and I never knew why. I was placed outside and told to scat. I didn't know where to find food or water and I had no idea where to find shelter. Day after day, I looked for my family but luck didn't seem to be on my side. Days turned into months and months turned into years.

I taught myself to hunt and I drank from puddles in the street. I never found shelter but I would hide beneath sheds or under a deck, trying to stay out of the harsh weather elements. It wasn't plush, but it helped me survive.

It's hard out here. I'm all on my own. I try to stay hidden nowadays, as it seems the best way to keep myself alive. When people do see me as I'm crossing the street, they try and speed up to run over my feet. Teens laugh and taunt me as I try to discretely stroll by. I try to act confident, but I'm really rather shy.

I try to camouflage myself in a bush when people will be walking by, but sometimes they spot me and I worry inside. Mostly they laugh, sometimes they point, other times they turn their head with a snort. No one seems to care about my plight for survival, so year after year, I cling to a dimming hope that someone might help me along for a while.

I'm tattered and torn. I'm weathered and scared. I'm hungry and scrawny and full of gray hair.

After years of trying my best to make it on my own, I feel my body giving up hope. Something inside tells me I'm breaking down and my heart doesn't fight it because I'm too tired now.

I found your house from the cat food bowl you keep on your porch. Thank you for the nourishment to keep us weary souls afloat. I saw that you spotted me outside yesterday. I perched on top of your fence; I had planned it that way. I know it's the end of the road for me and I'm just searching for a place that I can finally *be.*

I've watched you come and go for a few days and you seem so kind to other strays. Then, just today, you saw me again; my final plan was taking place like a gem. I wished I could have found you sooner, but fate led me to you now. If only I could communicate to you that I need you right now.

I'm tattered and torn, I'm old and I'm bruised. I'm fading away and need someone to see that I just need a place to rest. I promise I'll be no trouble at all. I just need a space that I can call my own.

Then the most miraculous event occurred. You held me and carried me inside in your arms. You gave me a room that I could call all my own; a buffet of food bowls lined the walls. A big fluffy blanket was given to me and that's when I knew it was meant to be.

You stroked my crumpled fur and I rested my head. That's when I knew I was nestled in love, for the first time in years, yet sadly, I knew my body was leaving this earth. You spoke to me with kindness and you comforted me as I passed. I wish I could thank you for your graciousness towards me. I wish I could tell you how much it meant to have found a place where I could finally rest.

Endless Love,

Charlie

## -The Printer-

# Dear Human Friend:

I'm elated that you have a home office!

While I do enjoy jumping into your recycling bin and hiding under a stack of used papers, what I most enjoy is when you use your printer. When the green button shines and the mechanism comes to life, I hop right onto the desk with my eyes peering into the machine. Paper is coming and it's moving fast!

There it is! Here it comes! Oh my - it's half way done. I promptly step on the sheet as it comes out from the machine. Uh oh, you're mad. Is it me? The paper is bunching as it pushes on through and now you're yelling- at me? Who knew?

I hop off the paper, now wrinkled and used. You shake your head – at me? I'm sorry for whatever I have done. I thought my job was to supervise the fun!

Now, I'll stand off to the side as you seem to demand. Here it comes, another page zooming out of the printer machine- I promise I won't sit on the sheet of paper this time. But I just can't avert my eyes. It's coming! There it is! A new page is coming our way! My eyes dart back and forth and watch the new page arrive. I did it! I've been good. I didn't sit on it this time. You smile with pleasure as you reach for the crisp page but just as you grab it my eyes dance with play. The paper, there it is, waving in the air. I can't help but jump and reach for it with my paw.

Oops my claw. I see that I've ripped the corner of your paper. Again, you shake your head in anger. I'm sorry! I look up at you with my eyes so cute; I didn't mean to cause a dispute!

You crumble the paper up into a ball and then toss it into the bin just for me to enjoy! I'm sorry you're having such a bad day, but I do appreciate the new toy which you've given me to play.

Thank you for loving me and giving me so much joy!

Many purrs,

Alana

# -Don't forget about me-

*Hi there.* You don't know me, but I want to introduce myself. I'm a senior cat and I don't know how I ended up here. Well, I do; but it's too hard to face. I miss having a home and a family. To be honest, I miss a lot of things.

My human family brought me into their home when I was a cute little kitten. I was full of energy and I loved to play. I lived with them as they introduced two children to our home and we all got along beautifully. We celebrated holidays together (I always helped open gifts by playing with the wrapping paper), we snuggled together on the couch nearly every night and on the rare occasion that I became sick, they took me to the doctor for good care. When my human family felt ill, I snuggled up extra close to them until they felt better- I wouldn't leave their side.

But it's been thirteen years and I'm not that cute little kitten anymore. But I'm still me! I'm just a bit older and slower now. I still love to snuggle, I'm still just as loyal as I've ever been. I still love my human family…even though they dumped me here and left me on my own.

I'm lonely and sad. Why did they leave me? What did I do wrong?

I don't know how much longer I have to live. Some people tell me cats only live an average of 14 years- so maybe I only have one year left. But the Guinness Book of World Records says a cat has lived to age 34…yes 34! Maybe that will be me? No one ever knows for sure how long they will live, but regardless of if I have one day left or several years, I still want to spend it surrounded by love.

No one wants to be dumped into a lonely metal cage to fade away in their senior years. All day I sit still like a good girl in my cage. I don't have much room to move and I overheard someone say my days were numbered. I'm scared. I hear stressed and barking dogs in the room next to me 24/7. I want to live. I want to be in a home. Why did my family dump me here? Where did they go?

I see you walking through the rows of cages today. You look like you're ready to adopt a feline friend. I know I'm so much older than everyone else here. I know I'm not tiny and full of endless energy. I'm not just learning to walk on my own. I do sleep a lot. But there are a lot of things I bring to the table, too. I love to snuggle and even though I don't know you yet, I promise if you save me- if you give me a forever home- I will be forever faithful to you. I will snuggle with you anytime. I won't knock over your holiday decorations. I won't tug at your window blinds. I will curl up in a sunny spot near the window. I will purr a lot and thank you every day for saving my life. I will be calm and easy going. I will take time to adjust, but I promise if you give me that time, I'll be so good.

I know I'm not that cute little kitten in the cage below me. I know I'm old. I know my time is limited. But please, don't overlook me.

When my family moved, they dumped me here. That's what the intake sheet noted. I saw it sitting on the counter as my family walked away for good. I know I'm just sitting here very still in my solitary cage. I know I am not hyper and tossing toys in the air for attention. But I'm sticking my paw through the bars trying to reach you now. Please don't forget about me. You can name me anything you choose. I'll be happy with any name you pick! I promise I'll be the best pet you've ever had…if you just give me a chance.

Love,

Shelter Feline #17259

## -Musical Cats-

# To my musical human:

I love when you play music on the piano. I sit next to you on the bench as you play, but after a few moments *I* want to play!

I like to step on the keys and hear the pretty notes.

But you never seem happy when I go rogue.

My music may not sound as beautiful as yours. I've never had lessons and am learning on the go.

Give me time, I'll keep practicing when you sit down to play.

One note, two notes…oh I think I'll just lie down. Oops- did you hear that? These darling piano keys make a really loud sound!

Bravo! Bravo! Keep playing your chords and reading your music, I'll just be here practicing in my own way. Please don't mind me; I'm not mad at sharing our practice time.

Lots of purrs,

Sparkles

## -Bedtime-

# My Dear Human:

You're brushing your teeth and the sky is dark. It's bed time! Hurray! It's bed time!

I jump into bed and pick a good spot. I think I'll choose the pillow tonight. I got my spot first! That's a victory, all right.

I watch as the others jump into bed, all grabbing a spot before you've come to rest your head. Next is Cooper the dog and then Winnie the cat. Oh wait- there's one more, it's Alison Pratt. She's older and bigger and moves pretty slow. But that doesn't stop her from joining our bed. We're all here together – now it's your turn to join.

I'm purring and cozy as I hear your footsteps grow near. "Where am I supposed to sleep?" I hear you exclaim. I quickly recoil and pretend not to hear. I guess the others are doing the same because no one moves a muscle as you sigh in defeat.

You climb into bed, one foot at a time. You twist and you turn to find space to call "mine". Finally, you're all curled up in a tight ball. You don't have a pillow because I'm using it tonight. You can touch your own toes because you've become so small, and Cooper the dog is spread out like a log! Winnie the cat is cozy and swell as she nestles up close to you and lets out a purr. Alison Pratt is just as well, she's chosen to curl up on your other side. *Swell.* Your arms are tucked under the blankets for warmth, but as you lie quietly wishing for sleep to come you realize your trouble. The cats have you trapped on each side of the covers. You're in a strait jacket of cats and your legs are bunched tight. Your head is hardly on the bed, your pillow already occupied.

You try to hold still and fall asleep through the vexation, but the longer you stay, the more frustrated you become. You want to stretch out your legs and to let your arms free. You want a pillow instead of giving it to me. You grunt as your temperature rises and you're desperate to move.

I'll give you *my* pillow, I decide. I'll give up my comfort for you tonight. I slowly stand and stretch out my legs. But I don't want to wake up, or give up my spot.

As I move away, your head quickly raises up to grab the pillow. You drift off to sleep quickly now and I giggle a little.

Now that you're sleeping, I can get cozy again. Oh! Whoops! Don't mind me, I'm just cozying in!

I try to walk softly but know I'm tugging on your hair. I slip and I stumble to find just the right spot. Once I've found it I go down; plop! I'm here! I'm okay! I've made it now.

I'm wrapped around the top of your head and purring again. Once I've settled, I hear you let out a groan. Your eyes open to glance up at me and close back on their own. Within no time at all, you've slipped your head back off the pillow and into a ball. Look at that; back to how we started! It was fate, after all!

Love,

Lydia

# -Harvey's Diary-

# Dear Diary:

Today my human was reading and I sat on her book. After trying to push me off the pages of the book, I finally laid down across the entire thing. Why in the world would she stare at a stack of paper when she can stare at me?

Love,

Harvey

## -Who Me?-

# Dear Loving Human:

I'm hiding behind the chair. I know you can't see me there. I watched you walk into your office and your eyes light up at the sight. I'm so sorry to have caused such a fright!

You were away from home and I was bored. I wandered into this room and began to play. It was truly harmless, I swear. I know I bunched up the rug and covered it in hair. I admit that next, I jumped up on your desk and scattered your papers around. Yes, a few even fell to the ground.

But the fun didn't stop there. I hopped and jumped and pushed down your chair. It made a loud boom as it fell to the floor, and that's when I ran behind the heavy door. The next thing I knew I heard your footsteps walk in. Oh dear! Oh my – he's going to be mad at me again!

Now, I'm hiding behind the old chair, hoping that you won't find me there. If I could fix the mess I've made, I would have been happy to hire a maid. But I can't fix it so I hid and hope you'll believe me when I say, it was the dog – it was him; he made your office this way!

Purrs,

chen

## -Cat Art-

**I did it again!** I think this work is my best yet. Oh, I can't wait until you come home to see what I've created! I wonder if you'll display my work for others to admire. I'm quite proud of this newly created art work and I hope you'll feel the same.

I created this piece with happiness at play!

I whittled and chewed. I bit and I clawed. My eyes danced with delight as I worked away. I kicked and I purred. I meowed and I growled- all to make you this art work today!

Hurray! You're home to see my display. I carry my art work by using my teeth and promptly drop it right at your feet.

"What did you do?" I hear you say. "You've made a mess while I've been gone all day!"

I push my art work towards you again and hope that you'll take a second look. I've worked all day to earn your praise.

But you only shake your head and say "My toilet paper. It's gone again. It's tattered and torn and I give in." It's true that the toilet paper has been used as my base. But I whittled and chewed and put everything in its place! It's art, I tell you and I'm not backing down. But I see your face now covered in a frown.

I only did it for you. Okay, a little for me. But I worked and worked like a busy bee. I shaped the roll of paper to be interesting, you see.

I guess some people just don't believe in art.

I'll try to give my art work a go again tomorrow while you're away at work.

Yours Truly,

Ginger, T.P. Cat Artist

## -Monday Morning-

**It's Monday?** It's raining? Okay…I think I'll do what I did yesterday.

Can you fill my food bowl before you leave for work?

Life is good.

-Alicia

## -Rubber Ducky-

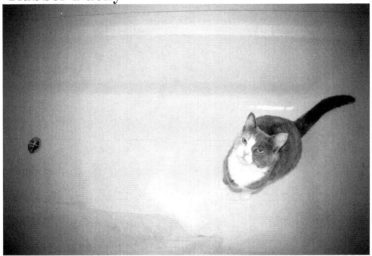

# Dear Diary:

My human caught me again. Yes, I admit it; I like to walk in the bathtub after she is done showering. I like to get my paws wet and lick them. I like to watch the water drain into the big circle near the top of the tub. But my human doesn't like me playing in the bathtub.

This time she caught me lying in the tub. I was lying on my back, all four paws in the air. I was getting my back wet. I wasn't doing any harm. Why can't I play in the tub? What's the harm in getting a little bit wet?

Today when I was caught, my human shook her head and said, all I need now is a rubber ducky. I don't know what that means, but she didn't seem pleased. I tried my best to act apologetic. I jumped out from the wet tub and rubbed her leg. But then she was mad because I got the bottom of her pants wet and some of my white fur rubbed off on her black pants too. *Oops!* I was only trying to be nice!

When she left for work, she left the door to the bathroom open. I knew she would be gone for a long time so I hopped back in the tub and walked back and forth again, getting my paws wet so I could lick them. She'll never know.

The only flaw in my plan? I fell asleep in the tub and she came home to find me there again. *Oops.*

Purrs,

Sunshine

**-Quiet-**

# Hey You:

I can't hear you. When you call my name I do not know.
When you ask me to come into the kitchen for my dinner I do
not know. When you yell at me for ripping the toilet paper
roll in the guest bathroom to shreds, again, I do not know.

I was born deaf. But between you and me, it's not so bad. I was adopted by a wonderful family and they've learned to communicate with me in a different way. Because I can't hear sounds, they use hand signals.

When it's time to wake up in the morning, I get so excited. I meow louder than any other cat. I don't know how loud I am meowing because I can't hear myself. But by the look on my human's faces, I think it must be VERY loud.

When I see the hand signal for dinner, I run as fast as I can to the kitchen and wait eagerly for my food.

When the doorbell rings or when the dogs start barking, I cannot hear them so I just walk calmly through the house. The other cats run to frantically hide beneath the couch. When the vacuum cleaner makes its appearance I do not hide then either. I am not scared, but the other cats seem to be.

So if you're visiting me, just remember, I can't hear what you're saying. I've learned that you don't need hearing to survive. If you have your health and you have love in your life- you are a rich purr-son. And I have both.

-Pearl

## -Why?-

# A question...

Why do we share our house with that big dog? I know he was here before I was...but I just don't understand the appeal. Let me lay it out for you...Cats versus Dogs.

*Cats*
+ You don't have to let us outside to go to the bathroom.
+ We bathe ourselves – no need for expensive grooming trips.
+ We don't bark when the doorbell rings—and really, we don't bark, ever!
+ You don't have to take us for walks- instead you can snuggle with us on the couch!
+ We can entertain ourselves with toys, boxes, a window to look outside...
+ We're small- we take up very little space!
+ We won't jump on you when you first get home – we'll wait until you come to us.

+ Our purrs have been said to have healing powers!
+ We don't need belly rubs. You can just pet us and we'll be happy to cuddle up close.
+ We can provide great entertainment when we are playing.

*Dogs*
… I tried. I'm sorry but I just can't think of any perks they have over cats.

So there you have it. Why do we have to share our home with a dog? He barks, he jumps, he knocks me over when he's hyper. You have to take him outside for walks in the rain and in the snow. You have to pick up after him when he goes potty outside *(ew!)*…do I really need to say any more?

Okay, I'm kidding. I love Cooper as much as you do. Maybe. But we all need to vent sometimes, right? The truth is he just came and ate all of my cat food- *every last morsel!* That big slobbery canine! Oh, but we say crazy things when we are hungry.

We can keep the dog. But seriously, can you come and fill up my food bowl now?

Love,

Snickers

## -The Porcelain Bowl-

# Dear Humans:

Thank you for bringing home a beautiful new water bowl for me. I know you keep one water bowl on each level of the house and that is so kind of you to do. But to be honest, my favorite water bowl is the one that's always been here.

You know the one- it's big and white. But sometimes you close the lid on it and I cannot get in to drink water when I need to.

Sometimes I even see you sit on it! (I'm not sure why you do that. I do not sit on *your* cups and glasses.)

Anyway, thank you for my water bowls…mostly thank you for the big porcelain one.

Love,

Buster

## -Bad Habits-

**I must confess...**the dog taught me these things:

The dog taught me to drink out of the toilet. If I don't do it, he will chase me throughout the house. I do it to please *him*.

The dog taught me to rub my wet nose all over the windows and on the glass door. He said you like the art work that it creates.

The dog taught me to chase my tail when I am bored. Sometimes when I'm done, I run into the wall from being dizzy. But the dog said it makes you laugh; and I do it- for *you*.

The dog taught me to beg for food. He uses his eyes to beg, but I found a better way. When you're eating dinner, I quietly climb under the table and place my claws in your leg. Generally, that gets your attention and some food will drop to the floor.

The dog taught me to jump on guests when they enter the front door. He said guests think it's cute when we do this. I must join in on the fun!

The dog taught me to protect our home from the mail carrier. I can't bark and when I see the mail carrier each day, I climb through the blinds, often getting tangled as I find my way to the window. I make sure to hiss and scare him away and every day it works. Once I hiss, he drops his papers and always walks (sometimes runs) away!

The dog also taught me to snuggle up close to you whenever you are sad or feeling down. He taught me that there is nothing more important in a family than being loyal to each other. While he may have taught me some "bad habits" he's also taught me some good ones- wouldn't you agree?

Thanks for giving us such a great home!

Love,

Mimi - & the dog

**-Ouch!-**

# Good Morning Humans!

It's time to get up! Get up I say! It's time to get up and start the day!

The sun is coming up and I'm ready to play. Why aren't you awake yet? It's time to get started on the day.

Hello? Good Morning? Open your eyes!

"Ouch" I hear you say as you wipe your hand over your face and swat me away.

Come on! Get up silly! Let's start our day!

I'm excited for a brand new day. I walk back and forth, sometimes pulling your long hair. Whoops, I just slipped. Did I scratch your face?

"My eyelid!" You cry as you sit up in bed.

You're awake! Hurray!

You give me a stern look and I widen my eyes. I'm sorry; I did not mean to catch your eyelid with my claw. But it's time to wake up and fill my bowl!

You're groggy and tired, but I'm eager to play. As your feet hit the floor, I dart off to my bowl.

Meow. Meow.

I'm waiting for you now. You're awake!

"You gave me a black eye!" You say. But then I hear your feet tip-toeing my way. You're coming to fill my empty bowl. I'm really sorry about your eye. Now it's breakfast time!

Good Morning! Hurray! It's such a great day!

Love,

Kiefer

## -Who Saved Who?-

# Dear people:

You saved my life many years ago. I was a stray trying my best to survive all alone on the streets. You took me in when I needed you most. You gave me water and food and shelter and love. You had me neutered and vetted and you promised me a life of joy.

Today when I saw you fall and begin to shake, I ran to your mom to lick her awake. I licked her face and licked her hands. I liked her toes and then she rose! I meowed and ran to you and she followed. That's when she saw you shaking. She called an ambulance and they came to the house. They saved you today.

I know I'm a cat and sometimes you even call me fat! But I'll always be grateful for what you did for me. I'll always be thankful for the home that you give me now, too. And for that, I did what I could today. I wanted to save your life as you saved mine.

I was left at home alone for most of the day and I've been so worried. But you've just returned and I'm so happy to see you again. I promise I'll always stay by your side. Because I'm a cat, I can't call 9-1-1, and I can't drive you to a hospital, but I can always find someone who can. I'll always be your right hand man!

Love,

Alex

## -The Plumber-

# Kind Sir:

I saw you trying to fix the sink yesterday. I heard you holler and shout and curse many times. I heard you say, the water won't drain.

And so...while you're away at work today I'm trying to tackle the problem. I've hopped on the counter and down into the sink. I stuck my head down the garbage disposal and even found a few old treats.

As I continued my work, I stuck each paw down the drain to examine it again. I pulled up a few extra noodles and then...

My head hit the lever that turns *on* the sink. Oh my! Now there's water gushing down. I drank a few licks and then started to worry. But to my amazement the water drained. Your sink is now working!

I'm magnificent! I'm great! I'm a dream come true…

When you come home I hope you'll think so too!

With Love,

vera

## -So Sorry!-

# Uh-Oh.

Please don't be mad! Remember you love me. I knocked over the garbage can while looking for something.

I know you said not to, and I'm sure you'll be mad. But I did it, it was me- I knocked over the can.

I was looking for that piece of chicken I saw you throw away after dinner last night. I could smell it, I could; it was just out of sight!

So I pushed off the lid and jumped in to investigate.

I searched and searched to no avail. But just as I found it, that's when I fell. I must have leaned over to one side too far! That trash can, it tumbled and over we went.

Don't worry, I grabbed the piece of chicken and ran just in time. But the other garbage fell all over the floor. Oh my! The dog came and nosed through the mess that I made. Then we both went on a search to find a maid.

So Sorry,

Nina

# -Narcolepsy-

Fjaklsjglkjkfah ateotieahgva vnvfjvnj
ahehtjkedgeatoooooooooooooooooo ahfhagj hjalkwew

Akfljriohgnaueuuuuuhgahghljeaepoj lkasgjaglkjea
awoigaegj wefkjlalkeajg ahowgheaga

Oops. I fell asleep on the keyboard again. I may need to have
that checked.

Purrs,

Marshall xoxo

## -Confession-

# Hey There.

It was me.

I ate your paper while you slept last night. I tried, but I couldn't resist the temptation.

I know you had written a note on that paper. I don't know what it said, please don't ask me- you should know already, cats cannot read. But the paper made a crinkling noise when I touched it with with my paw. I tried, but I just couldn't resist…

I pawed at the paper and listened to the noise and then chased it around the room, skidding on all fours. I threw it in the air and took a big bite. I felt so tough hunting that paper last night!

So I admit, it was wrong. But I had so much fun!

Please remember, next time you want to buy me a new toy; I now prefer balls of paper, they provide endless joy!

Your Blissfully Happy Cat,

Ashle

# -Tears-

## My Human:

I saw you crying on your pillow last night. I jumped on your bed and curled myself around your head.

I don't know what made you so somber, but whatever it is, I'm here now. I'll purr and snuggle close to you as long as you need me to.

Much Love,

cait

## -Passing-

# To my rescuer:

You saved me five years ago when no one else would. I was living in unspeakable conditions and as an unaltered cat living among many others, I gave birth time and again before you came to save me that day. When you rescued me, I was old. When you took me to the veterinarian they were more than alarmed at my condition. My kidneys were half of the size they were supposed to be. My teeth were rotted. My hair had fallen out. My eyes were swollen with severe infections. I was terribly emaciated. Yet despite how I looked and despite the diagnosis I was given- you saved me.

I lived with you for five happy years. I tried my best to show you how much I appreciated your kindness. I carried my toys to you and meowed as I placed them at your feet while you were working. I ran up and rubbed your ankles every time you came home. I snuggled with you when you read a book or watched a movie.

And then in the blink of an eye, five years flew by. Suddenly my age caught up to me and I knew I was fading fast. You sat next to me and rubbed my head. I pawed my soft pillow and purred. I didn't want to go; I loved my life with you. I wanted very much to stay, and I was thankful to you again as you sat beside me in those final moments. I rested my head next to your leg and focused on your fingers petting my soft fur. As I took my last breath I heard you say how much you loved me and I hope you know how much I loved you too. You were everything to me because you gave me life. You rescued me from the unthinkable. You shared five wonderful years with me. You taught me that humans can be kind and life can be good. Against all odds, I survived because of you.

I would have died where I was trying to survive and the animal shelter would have killed me in an instant. But you looked past all of that and saved me when no one else would. A special needs senior cat that needed ongoing medical care; you were the one who was always there.

Last night I passed away as you sat next to me. But I wanted to leave this note and say thank you for all you did. Because of you my life was happy. Because of you I kept my tail held high. Because of you, I knew love. So this note is simply to say, thank you, *for being you.*

Love Always,

Ruby

**-Mistakes Happen-**

# Dear Guardian:

Today while you were away at work, I tore a hole in the window screen. I admit it was me. I won't try and blame *this* on the dog; I take full credit for this mishap. I do. But before you get upset, please let me explain…

A small flock of birds flew up next to the window and they were taunting me. They flapped their wings and looked at me through the screen. I heard them squawking. They knew I couldn't reach them through the barrier of the screen. I tried to restrain myself, I promise I tried. But they just kept hovering by the window and looking in at me. I chattered my teeth and twitched my tail. At one point, I even let out a little meow. But they didn't heed my warnings, so I feel it's really their fault. After twenty-minutes of heckling me, I lost it. In a moment of weakness, I leapt towards the window and began to claw. The dog barked, knowing I should stop but I just couldn't. Before I knew it, I tore a hole in the screen and the flock of birds flew away. Only then did I realize the joke was on me.

The birds got away safely but I was left with a torn window screen, knowing you would be mad at me.

So I'm sorry for this mishap, I truly am. I promise you I won't do it again. The birds got the best of me; what can I say? I can't believe they kept laughing at me as they all flew away.

I can't fix the screen for you because, well, I am a cat. But please remember it was just a minor mishap! We all make mistakes- I know I've heard you say this, too. (Don't forget about the time I saw you sneak an early bite of fondue!)

Love,

Mallory

## -Dear Editor of the Newspaper-

# Dear Editor:

I turn 5 years old today. I should be hearing HAPPY BIRTHDAY but instead I only hear the silence of an empty animal shelter that no one wants to visit. The employees forget to feed us, my litter box is never scooped. My water bowl is collecting dust. No one here knows it is my birthday. No one seems to care.

Once upon a time I heard Happy Birthday on this celebrated day. But today, I hide in the back of a dark steel cage, alone, cold, hungry, thirsty and terribly sad. I think the employees forgot about me. Can adopters even find me in this dark and stuffy room?

I don't know if I'll ever hear those two blissful words again. It's okay if no one ever knows my birthday again. But it's not okay if I die here. I long for someone to adopt me and love me. If birthday wishes are real things, that's what I wish for- a home. I long to hear the word CONGRATULATIONS more than anything as I travel to my forever home.

I'm writing this letter to the paper today to ask you to consider adopting me. I promise I'll be a great addition to your home. I promise I'll be on my best behavior. I promise.

I hope to meet you soon.

Love,

Maxine

## CAT SEEKING LAP

Young single black & white spayed female seeks human (aka adopter) for late night chats, snuggling, petting and brushing. Hoping to find a match that is full of love!

## -CONTACT TESSA-

-PET PERSONALS-

## CAT SEEKING LOVE

Middle-aged beauty with slight grooming

obsession seeks loving human (aka adopter) who

enjoys endless snuggling. I have a lot of love

to share!

## -CONTACT SUNNY-

## -PET PERSONALS-

## CAT SEEKING COMPANION

Recent young empty-nester with incredibly friendly demeanor seeking human (aka adopter) to enjoy evening television shows, good books, and/or daytime play dates.

## -CONTACT REGINA-

-PET PERSONALS-

## CAT LOOKING FOR CONNECTION

Extremely loving spayed female seeks

human (aka adopter/forever family) who

enjoys playing with cat toys, petting me and

LOTS of snuggle time!

## -CONTACT PUMPKIN-

# -CHAIN LETTER-

# Dear Recipient:

This is a chain letter that originated from a former foster cat. I am passing it along to 25 people. I am told by the sender of this letter that if I forward this note along, I will receive $1000 in the mail, within 2 weeks. I'm hoping it's true. I would love to purchase some cat nip, a big cozy cat bed and then maybe I could use some of the left over money to buy a new couch for my humans (I sort of scratched it pretty badly over the past year!). So cross your whiskers, cross your paws and send this chain letter onto 25 people!

Purrs,

Darla

## -Santa Paws-

# Dear Santa Paws:

I've been really well behaved this year. Last year, I know I had a few issues: I scratched up the furniture, I urinated on my new pet bed (I wasn't fond of the color), I barfed in a shoe and I tore the pages of an open book to shreds. But this year I behaved, I promise.

This year, I changed my ways. When I had a hairball, I left it in the sink. When I got a new pet bed and it was *(eh!)* plaid, I just ignored it and sat on the couch instead. When I saw the newspaper sitting on the coffee table and I wanted to shred it, I resisted the urge and went to play with my barrel of cat toys instead. See, I told you I've been good! So this year my holiday wish list is: a window perch, a big tub of cat nip, a PINK pet bed and a big empty box to play in.

Happy Holidays!

Lots of purrs,
Chewbacca

-Dear Diary-

# Dear Diary:

I bit my human's big toe when he was sleeping. It was just a nibble, really. I didn't mean any harm; I was just curious.

Marsha

-Yes, I ate that-

## Note to Self:

I ate a full 6-inch sub sandwich today. My guardian walked away from her desk and headed to the other room. I swooped in and gobbled up the entire sandwich within minutes. It was delicious. Turkey and cheese. I ate all 6-inches, in record time.

This is a reminder: stay close when sandwiches are near!

Miss America

## -Oh, Roommates!-

# Dear Roomie:

Living with humans can be a bit of a challenge. Don't get me wrong, I am totally grateful for all that you do. You fill my food and water bowls' each morning. You keep a warm cozy house for us, and goodness do I love those sunny windows. But as roommate's, we should set a few boundaries. I have outlined my ideas below:

- Let's not go overboard with dry food. Feed gourmet wet food to me every morning and evening.
- The fluffy pillow on the bed belongs to the cat.
- Leave the bathroom sink slightly dripping ( it's great entertainment).
- Leave the television on when you're away from the house. I prefer MTV, please.

Just a few little things; easy-peasy! How does this sound to you?

Love Always,

Albert

## -My Dream Job-

# Dear Journal:

I've always wished to be a writer. But my cat friends laugh at me and ask me what a cat would ever write about. I have lots of ideas. Stories of chasing mice, creating mischief around the house and stories of meeting other foster cats like me.

I once heard someone say that you can do anything your heart desires. And I was named after a children's author, after all. Maybe I'll put together a book of letters from the cat's I've met along my journey to adoption; there's an idea!

XO,

Eve Bunting

# Dear Cat:

Passing notes to you is fun and after you read this note we can tear it to shreds and slide across the hardwood floors. I just wanted to say I'm glad you're here. I know we both had tough starts in life. You came from an animal shelter and I was a homeless cat living on the streets. But look at us now! What a difference a year can make. We're living the good life. We have food every day, fresh water, lots of fun toys and we have people to snuggle with. Sometimes I wonder how we got so lucky.

Anyway, I wanted to pass this note to you to say I love you. I know we bicker and argue sometimes, but I'm glad we have each other. Now let's shred this note before the humans see it!

~Andy

# -Taylor Swift-

# Dear Miss Taylor Swift:

I love your Coke commercial. Every time you take a sip of your drink, more cats appear by your side. I would love to star in your next commercial! You sang a song about me once- *Lucky One*! It's my favorite song, of course. Please tell your cats: Meredith and Olivia Benson I said hello!
Tootles,
Lucky

**-The Shame Game-**

"I poop on the couch when I'm mad."

I leave dead mice in their shoes when I'm happy.
But when I'm mad, I poop on the couch.
-T.J.

**-More Shaming-**

I tinkle in the bathtub after you leave.
-Marley

-Feral Friends-

## Dear Colony Caretaker:

We depend on you and we're so thankful for you. You put
out fresh food and water every day to help us nourish our
bodies. You had us all spayed and neutered and we're so
much healthier now. Even better, we've stopped reproducing
which means there is enough food for all of us, and the
community where we live is happy knowing that our colony
will fade through attrition rather than repopulate by the
hundreds.

You brought us warm huts filled with straw for those cold
winter nights; saving our ears from painful frostbite. Your

kindness does not go unnoticed. We all appreciate your efforts more than you will ever know.

We only peer out at you from behind cars and bushes- but we know you're there and we love you. We are feral cats so we won't allow you to touch us; we like our outdoor home. Even though we're not cuddly cats, we're still grateful for your help. It is because of you that so many good things have happened to our colony. One person can make a difference when they're committed to understanding feral cats.
So thank you, beyond words. Thank you for saving our lives. Thank you for coming each day.

-Ziggy & pals

## -Moving Day-

## Attention Humans:

It's moving day! Thank you for taking us with you. I know you found us as strays living beneath your porch last month. You didn't have to save us; but you did. And now we're spayed and healthy and we're moving with you! Thank you for helping us when no one else would. Thank you for opening up your home to save three orphaned sisters. Thank you for all that you do.

Much Love,

Rae, Roo, and Ree

**-The Breakfast Club-**

# Dear Purrson:

You know, I've always been particularly loyal to you since the day you took me in. But today, I'm leaving you this secret note to let you in on something more. I know you know that I'm well behaved all of the time. But my housemates aren't always that way. As the oldest and most mature of our crew I thought I should share the *true* on-goings of our house with you:

- Sally sleeps on the stove top all day long and I know you don't allow us on the counter tops.
- Dory shreds the toilet paper in the guest bathroom…*every day*.
- Larry rubs his nose on all of the windows- leaving smudge marks everywhere.
- Larry also scratches on the back of the couch…with his claws.

Please don't tell the others I told you.

-Magoo

P.S. This is Larry and I'm adding this note to let you know that Magoo isn't as good as he pretends to be. Today he left a hairball in your fancy dress shoe. Just thought you should know.

## -For the Fosters-

# Dear Foster Family:

I understand that I'm here for a temporary stay. Thank you for inviting me into your happy abode. I've never known so many joys.

I once slept in a damp sewer drain. Now I sleep on a warm fluffy bed.

I once was cold and alone. Now I curl up by the warmth of the fireplace and I'm surrounded with love and laughter.

I once was shot at, chased and kicked on the streets. Now I'm petted and cherished and have a warm lap to sleep in.

I once was starving and unsure of where to find my next meal. Now you fill my bowls with daily nourishment and I never have to worry.

I once became pregnant- over and over again- always fearing for my kittens lives and my own. Now I am spayed, healthy and in good health.

I once peered inside of windows to homes like yours- dreaming of a different life. Now I *have* that dream life.

I know I'm not your forever pet, but I'm happier than I've ever been. You tell me that one day I'll find a forever family to call my own, and I know I can believe you. And until that day comes, I get to remain with you.

Because you were kind enough to open your home to me- a feline soul in need; because you were willing to give me a chance, to feed me, love me and welcome me- because of you I now know how great life can be. Because of you, I have everything.

And when my adoption day arrives, I hope you'll always know how much you've meant to me. You'll be forever in my heart and soul; a savior that I can always know is mine.

Love,

Erica

# -Letter to my Rescue Cats-

## Dear Rescue Cats:

Permanent cats, foster cats, feral cats and stray cats – I care about all of you dearly. I wish you each a lifetime of happiness and love. When you are initially rescued, I know you are terrified and unsure of your future. Thank you for trusting me after all you've been through. Many of you have endured unthinkable pasts; abuse, neglect, facing certain shelter death, being tossed out on the street to fend for yourselves…I know what you've faced is unimaginable. I can see it in your eyes and your actions as you enter our doors. But over time and with patience and work, you blossom into the most trusting of souls.

Although I know I've helped you find life when it seemed to nearly come to an end, you've helped me too. But where do I begin?

You've helped me learn (and reminded me when needed)…

- To be grateful for the little things in life (a smile, a laugh).

- To live each day to the fullest.
- To be silly when the mood strikes.
- To rest when rest is needed.
- To vocalize my concerns.
- To be loyal.

While I'm grateful for all that you have taught me, I also have a few questions for you...

- Why do (only) the white cats rub against my black dress pants just before I'm about to leave for a meeting?
- When you have a hairball, why do you always insist on having it on my laptop? Have you made this location a universal rule among you?
- Why do you insist on sleeping on my head?
- When I'm walking with an overloaded basket full of laundry, why must you always race me down the stairs?
- When I feed you your daily treat of canned cat food why must you swat at me (using your claws)?
- When I (or guests) go to the bathroom, why do you scratch furiously under the bathroom door?
- Why do you always sit on my book when I'm reading? Why can't you sit next to me instead?
- When I place the magazines on the living room table- why must you bite the edges of each and every cover?

I can see from your letters that you have questions for me too. But despite all of the queries, I love you all. I do!

Love,
Stacey

# SPECIAL DEDICATION TO
## feline foster families, everywhere

# THANK YOU!

Thank you to YOU, the reader, for making *Letters from Cats: Hilarious and Heartfelt Notes,* a reality! A portion of proceeds from book sales will be donated to Ohio Spay & Neuter. Ohio Spay & Neuter is a program of Advocates 4 Animals, Inc. – a 501(c)3 non-profit organization. Their mission is to end pet homelessness in Ohio, through providing humane education and affordable spay and neuter options for cats and dogs.

If you share your home with a rescued cat, a senior cat or a special needs cat – thank you. And thank you to feline foster parents from coast to coast; you are truly life-savers.

Much gratitude to my wonderful editor, Gloria Rayle. Thank you to Rockville Publishing, for collaborating on another feline focused book. **More than 70% of cats who enter United States animal shelters are killed, and anything we can do to bring attention to this epidemic is much appreciated.**

Advocates 4 Animals, Inc.
*Rescue/Adoption * Spay/Neuter * Pet Food Pantry*

# ABOUT
# ADVOCATES 4 ANIMALS

Advocates 4 Animals, Inc. is a 501(c)(3) non-profit organization. Our mission is to end feline neglect and homelessness through a variety of programs such as our Pet Food Pantry, Spay It Forward Program, Feral Cat Program and our Rescue/Adoption Program.

All donations are tax-deductible and go directly to the animals. Every dollar donated truly makes a difference in helping to save lives in urgent need. Thank you for your kindness, compassion and support of animals in need.

To learn more or donate today, please visit:
*www.Advocates4Animals.com*

**\*Note:** A portion of proceeds from the sale of this book will be donated to Ohio Spay & Neuter.

# ABOUT
# OHIO SPAY & NEUTER

Ohio Spay & Neuter's mission is to end pet homelessness in Ohio, through providing humane education and affordable spay/neuter options.

All donations are tax-deductible and help support spay/neuter programs throughout the state of Ohio.

Learn more: *www.OhioSpayandNeuter.com*

# MEET THE AUTHOR

Stacey Ritz is a pet expert, blogger, award-winning author/writer, Ritz is also the Executive Director and Co-Founder of Advocates 4 Animals, Inc., a 501(c)3 feline welfare organization. Ritz often finds herself perplexed in the midst of comical situations that warrant sharing. Read her daily musings at *KittiesInTheCity.com* or *Advocates4Animals.com*.

Stac, as she's most often called, recently realized, spelled backwards, her name is "cats." Ironic? Maybe not.

**<u>DID YOU ENJOY THIS BOOK?</u>**
**IF SO, PLEASE LEAVE AN AMAZON REVIEW!**

## OTHER BOOKS BY STACEY RITZ

*Pawsitive Connection:*
*Heartwarming stories of animals finding people when we*
*need them most - Volume I*

*Covered in Pet Fur:*
*How to start an animal rescue, the right way*

# Covered in
# Pet Fur

## How to Start an Animal Rescue
## *The Right Way*

**STACEY RITZ** *and* **AMY BEATTY**
**Founders of Advocates 4 Animals**

**YOUR FREE SAMPLE CHAPTER OF *COVERED IN PET FUR***

*Covered in Pet Fur: How to Start an Animal Rescue, The Right Way.*
Stacey Ritz and Amy Beatty.
Published by Rockville Publishing

Front cover photo courtesy of Advocates 4 Animals, Inc.
Back cover photo courtesy of GCPS

ISBN: 978-1507557273

PRINTED IN THE UNITED STATES OF AMERICA

**TABLE OF CONTENTS**

# FORWARD

IT SAT IN A FORGOTTEN PART OF THE CITY. The dilapidated building was dark and surrounded by an eight foot tall barbed wire fence. The only sign was no larger than a sheet of computer paper. It was crookedly suspended, hanging from one rotting corner just above the padlock. It read "OPEN HOURS" and any remaining words had been long since bleached by the relentless sun. I double checked the address on my sheet of paper. (This was before I owned a cell phone and I had never dreamed that one day we would have GPS systems leading us anywhere we desired to go.) It was the correct address. But weren't animal shelters supposed to be friendly places filled with people who adored animals? Weren't non-profit organizations supposed to be clean and welcoming? Weren't they there to help? My mind buzzed with questions, although neither of us said a word. We were still in undergraduate school learning the ways of the world. Yet we had no idea we were about to embark on one of our most impactful lessons as we hesitantly approached the padlocked gates.

A burley man in a blue and black checkered flannel vest strolled out to the fence from inside, a worn cigarette hanging from the left corner of his mouth as a cloud of smoke surrounded his solemn face. I admit I wanted to turn and run back to the safety of our car. But my curiosity got the best of me. Or maybe we were both just paralyzed; in shock from our new surroundings. We were accustomed to our plush college campus, bright lights, clean sidewalks, smiling faces…but somehow we had driven ourselves just a few miles away into what felt like the Twilight Zone. Maybe now, well over a decade later, I would have turned and run. No seriously, who I am kidding? I would have stayed. I wanted to know what was behind the barbed wire. I wanted to know what happened to the animals who were found being abused, who were no longer wanted through no fault of their own. I wanted to know the reality of life for companion animals in our country. And although we spent years volunteering at various shelters, pounds and sanctuaries around the Midwest, I attribute what we have built today to our first day at this particular shelter; where countless lives were tossed into the dark and left, forgotten by the rest of the world. *Out of sight, out of mind.*

We located the shelter address through the phone book. I am well aware that this dates us, as we were living in a pre-Google time. But maybe what saved us was my chatter. I'll never be sure, but back in those days I tended to ramble when my nerves got the best of me. It was my own way of trying to calm myself. Whatever it was, the flannelled man we came to know as Todd pulled out his key and allowed us through the gates and into the city shelter. Our bewildered faces tried to take it all in. When we explained that we wanted to volunteer, Todd raised his eyebrows as if to indicate that we must be crazy. He explained that he did not have any open paid positions, not understanding why anyone would subject themselves to this environment without receiving a paycheck. We told him we just wanted to spend time with the animals, to bring in toys for the cats, to take the dogs on walks; we just wanted to give them some love and attention while they waited behind bars for a slim chance at finding a home. Todd nodded, clearly thinking we would never return.

First, Todd led us to a narrow building they called "the cat room". Small rusty wire cages were piled from floor to ceiling and stacked side by side. Only a slender opening existed down the center of the piles of cages leaving a space for us to walk. No one was spayed or neutered. No one was vaccinated. A few animals had food in their cages, hardly any had water and the bowls looked as if they had been dry for quite some time. No one had toys and most of the litter boxes were overflowing with old feces. Many cats started meowing when we entered the room, some stuck their paws through the wire bars, begging for help. My initial reaction was to run and open every cage door and let them all run free in the room while we scrambled to clean their cages and fill their bowls with fresh food and water and their crates with toys and clean litter. But instead I pressed my hands behind my back and tried to remain calm. We asked questions about how many adoptions they had, why absolutely no vetting was supplied to the pets in their care and we learned that there had never been volunteers. *Never.*

Next we walked over to the main building. The room looked to be caving in and the small space was dark. No natural light existed. It looked more like an old barn than a shelter. There was no heating or air conditioning, just cages stacked in endless rows, filled with dogs of every color and size. Most of them couldn't stand up in their cages without having to hunch down in their cramped quarters. The dogs never left their crates unless by some odd stroke of luck they were adopted by a rare visitor. Todd said the only other way the dogs ever left their cages happened to be if they died in their crates, and that happened too often. There were six long rows of wire dog crates lining what we grew to call The Warehouse. The crates were stacked on top of each other, just as the cats had been. Only with the dogs, some small dogs were caged next to large dogs and they fought viciously through the bent metal bars, frustrated by their helpless fates. It was enough to rattle even the most placid visitors. It wasn't until months later that we would learn of a "secret room" in a back building where additional dogs were held in the dark. This building was more like a shed. Like The Warehouse it had no natural light, but to make matters worse, there was no electricity and the cage floors had rotted, leaving the dogs behind bars often yelping in pain as their paws fell through the rotted holes in the floor boards.

We began volunteering once a week and then twice. Every free moment we had outside of classes, studies and our training and competitions for the indoor track, outdoor track and cross country team we found ourselves driving to the forgotten corner of town and spending hours upon hours with the imprisoned animals.

Todd left us to our own devices. He stayed in his small building off to the side from the others. We would always stop in and say good-bye as we left each time and he would be leaning back in his chair puffing away on that old cigarette. As ghastly as it may sound, more than a decade and a half later, Todd is still the most compassionate open intake shelter or pound director we have met to date. I wish it wasn't so, but Todd shines above the others we would meet as time marched on. Compassion, among other things, somehow is always missing in our nation's city shelter and county pound directors. Job requirements tend to be focused on obedience and adherence to the random stipulations of keeping the cages empty at all costs, rather than trying to help the animals that the facility should be there to serve and protect.

By our second visit to the dilapidated shelter, we had opened every cat cage in the room, letting them run free. The cats had a window and each took turns looking out into the world, some perhaps for the first time in years. A few cats jumped on top of the long heavy lights hanging from the ceiling and knowing they were happy to move around, we laughed in delight. We made hundreds of toys so that every cage had several variations to help numb the sting of solitude when they were locked back up and we were away. Each visit we thoroughly cleaned every litter box and gave them fresh food and water. We lined their wire crates with newspaper so that their paws could find a soft place to land (we would collect old newspapers and bring them with us). We were college students and didn't have much extra money, but when we had some to spare we would buy treats to give the cats on our visits. In time we developed a system where every visit, we let ten cats out of their cages at a time to play, rotating until everyone had a taste of freedom for the day. On rare occasion Todd would walk over to the small building and crack the door open to ask if everything was going okay. He may have thought we were crazy, two twenty-year olds spending our free time playing with cats; but we didn't think a thing about it. We were exactly where we wanted to be.

After spending half of the day with the cats, we would move on to the dogs. For the first few months of volunteering we would choose five dogs to walk at once. We would secure them into collars and leashes and take off into the city surrounded by fast moving cars with tinted windows and booming music, and strolling through deserted parks. We would walk the group of dogs for a mile or so and head back for another batch. We walked Pit-Bulls and Rottweiler's, Chihuahua's and mixed breeds. At the time we didn't know the labels given to any of the breeds; we only knew that they needed exercise and fresh air. We knew intuitively that they needed love.

Eventually we discovered a large fenced area in the back of the buildings. The grass was tall and the area had clearly never been used. *Another forgotten place.* Our young minds saw the unused space as an opportunity. That very day, without asking permission, we giggled like children as we took the dogs from their unsightly cages one by one and released them into the fenced back yard. After an hour we had every dog from the shelter out in the yard together. It never occurred to us that some dogs may not get along with others. It never crossed our minds that most of the dogs were unaltered. We only knew we wanted them to experience life, rather than to simply rot away in the forgotten building. If we could bring them one good day, we knew they would be happier for it. We didn't have any dog toys, but we found old branches and tossed them to the larger dogs. We kneeled on the ground to pet the small and senior canines and our eyes danced as we watched every one of them trot and run in the forgotten space, taking in the fresh air that touched their bodies, some for the first time in years. Todd wandered out into the yard after hearing our shouts of play and I turned just in time to see him shake his head, that darn cigarette hanging permanently from the corner of his mouth. Before I could blink, he had disappeared back into his office and we continued to play.

In all of our years at the shelter, we continued the tradition of letting the dogs run free together in the yard while we played with them and gave them attention (and we did the same for the cat room). Never once did we encounter an altercation between the dogs. They loved the sweet taste of freedom and it was clear that they weren't going to do anything to lose those moments of rare bliss.

During our last two years of undergraduate school, we scheduled a date once a year where the entire women's track team came to volunteer at the city animal shelter. Some spent time with cats and others helped walk the dogs throughout the city.

We continued volunteering several times a week as the years marched on and we grew closer to earning our degrees. We flew to Stanford, rode charter buses to Duke and everywhere in between for our competitive races (track and cross country) and each time we returned, we found ourselves covered in pet fur in a forgotten corner of the city. One day as we entered the cat room, we noticed an elderly cat who stood motionless in her rusty cage, a malnourished kitten draped lifelessly over her boney back. The older cat had long brittle gray fur that fell off in clumps with each new breath. One eye held steady on us, the other was missing and left in its place was a socket full of fresh oozing blood and infection. We reached in to hold her and felt every bone in her frail body. The little beige kitten wasn't fairing any better. We carried them across the gravel yard and into Todd's office to ask about them. Where had they come from? What happened to the older ones eye? Couldn't they get some veterinary care? By that point we had been talking with veterinarians in the area to see if they would be willing to donate some of their time to the forgotten shelter. We were dismissed as "dumb kids" time and again, until one veterinarian said *maybe*. That maybe got us fired up. We pitched the idea to Todd and he said it wasn't possible. We tried time and again to bring veterinarians to the shelter. We offered to drive shelter pets to the veterinarian's office. We offered everything we could think of to allow the shelter pets to be provided at least the minimal forms of veterinary care, but our efforts were to no avail.

The frail, elderly one-eyed gray cat had been turned in a few days before, Todd explained. Their best guess was that someone had purposely gouged her eye out. The kitten who was with her wasn't hers; they just didn't have anywhere else to place him. And so the two numb souls sat huddled together in a bottom cage, waiting for…nothing. No veterinary care was coming. No one would adopt either sick cat. They were simply waiting to rot away like the building itself had been doing for years before our arrival.

"Could we adopt them?" I blurted out instinctively. Todd shrugged his shoulders nonchalantly.

"Sure, just need to see your driver's license. That old one, she won't make it another night." He took a long puff of his cigarette as he filled out a yellowed piece of paper. "You can have her for free. She'll never make it."

We clung to the two cats, knowing if we adopted them, we could take them in for desperately needed veterinary care. And a minute later, we found ourselves saving our first two shelter cats – embarking on what would soon evolve into Advocates 4 Animals, Inc.

We named the elderly gray cat Princess. After taking the frail cat to a veterinarian and spending $500 on surgery for her gouged eye, my parents stopped talking to me. Clearly unhappy with how I choose to spend the minimal money I had as a college student, they shook their heads in disapproval. A month later we shelled out a few hundred dollars more for Princess as it was discovered her uterus was falling apart internally. We had her spayed and vaccinated and each day she grew stronger. Her hair grew in healthy and full, she threw her tail in the air as she trotted through the house and after more than a month of coaxing her to eat, she finally began eating on her own. Her emaciated 4-pound adult body grew into a healthy 12-pounds. Princess inspired our logo for Advocates 4 Animals and despite all that she had endured, despite the dire warning Todd had given us that Princess would not last one more night, she lived 10 more years.

Sadly the kitten we saved with her passed away within a week. In his severely malnourished state, he had been given a strong dose of adult flea preventative at the shelter, which had ultimately killed him. Although no vetting was provided at the shelter, the flea medications had been delivered as a promotion and shelter workers had not been versed on how to administer the medications (the adult version was too strong for his weak kitten body).

We saved a handful of others from that particular shelter prior to moving away from the city after college graduation, and we hung posters and flyers on every free light post and telephone pole encouraging others to adopt a rescue pet as well. Adoptions at the shelter saw an increase and we were pleased knowing that this was a step forward. Sadly, the shelter never forged a relationship with a veterinarian. Todd left the shelter the year after we had graduated and moved out of state. A few years later we learned that the forgotten shelter had been condemned. As for us, we continued leading a life covered in pet fur. After countless years spent volunteering in shelters, pounds, sanctuaries and working at various veterinary hospitals, kennels and operating a pet-sitting business we pressed on to co-found an organization that existed to specifically help shelter pets in need. We set out to reform the shelter system. We were two girls on a mission of compassion, a mission of humane treatment for the millions of voiceless victims needlessly dying in shelters and pounds each year through no fault of their own. And today, that mentality hasn't changed. We're still two girls, albeit a bit older now, on a mission to transform the grim reality of shelter pets into one of a reality of thriving existence. We're still fighting the same battles, one shelter and pound at a time. We're initiating viable programs to combat the tired mentality of shelter and pound directors who continue to embrace killing as a method of population control.

We've helped transform high-kill shelters into No Kill facilities, one at a time. In our own county, we've worked relentlessly for more than 11 years to try and work with our own county pound (which saves a mere 18% of healthy, friendly cats who enter their doors each year). After more than a decade of persistence, we're now the first approved rescue to be given permission to pull death row cats from this facility. But we still have a long way to go. After more than a decade of operating Advocates 4 Animals, we have established a handful of robust programs to combat our local pound's tired and outdated policies. Collaboration is generally the best route for helping the animals, but when you have a slaughter house (aka high-kill county pound) that refuses to embrace *any* life-saving measures, you do your best to keep animals out of their "care" by any and all means. Over the years, in addition to our rescue/rehabilitation/adoption program, we have established a pet food pantry to provide temporary pet food assistance to families facing financial hardship. By providing pet food, families are able to keep their pets with them, rather than relinquish them to the pound and a terrible fate. We have established an affordable spay/neuter program for cats within our own county, again to help humanely control the pet population and to keep pets from being turned in to the pound. We have a Community Cats program which works to train and assist the public in TNR (trap-neuter-release) for feral cats. These, among other programs are helping us lower the rate of animals entering the local pound; therefore decreasing the number of needless deaths perpetuated by that very pound.

Across the country, additional animal rescue/adoption, spay/neuter program and pet food pantry programs are urgently needed. One of the most popular questions we are asked is "How can I start a rescue?" It's not a simple one-word answer. If you do it right, you are actively helping animals in need. It may look "easy" to those on the outside, but as with anything worth doing, the endeavor of creating a non-profit (i.e. for purpose) animal welfare organization is filled with endless hard work, dedication, compassion, and perhaps most importantly a strong business sense. Yes, operating an animal rescue or animal welfare organization is a business. If you're considering starting an animal rescue organization you must have a plan in place and you must operate as a business.

The chapters ahead outline the basics of what you'll need to consider prior to starting an organization of your own. While the need for helping animals is ever present, the need for creating a viable, sustainable organization is essential. Don't fret: if you do not want to start your own organization and you're simply interested in understanding more about animal rescue this book is for you too! Whether you wish to help one or two animals a year through fostering for an organization, or you hope to start your own organization, this book is for you. The chapters ahead share the fundamental elements necessary to start an animal welfare organization *the right way*. In addition, we share our own experiences with you along the way. From hilarious mishaps to tough lessons, we share some of our most memorable stories throughout the book in hopes of helping you find your own path toward helping animals in need. Although everyone's journey will be unique, we can promise you one thing; if you devote even a portion of your life to helping animals in need, you will, at times be blissfully covered in pet fur.

**SPECIAL NOTE:** Many chapters in this book are followed by a "challenge" page which consists of both thought-provoking and action seeking questions to consider in regard to your own community and the animals you wish to help.

## CHAPTER 1: PAWS & CONSIDER THE FACTS...

WHILE WAITING ON A FOSTER HOME SPACE to become available, we asked the Good Samaritans who contacted us at Advocates 4 Animals to help a mom cat and her newborn babies, if they could safely keep her inside of their home until we had an opening two days later. They agreed and we were happy to have space to help. We work to save death row shelter pets on a daily basis and we work to combat cats ever entering the shelter through our rescue/adoption program. All of our foster/adoptable pets are housed in individual volunteer foster homes and the number of lives we can save is always dependent on the number of quality, trained foster homes we have in our network. The constant pressure to help is enormous as it comes from pet guardians wanting to surrender their pets for one reason or another, from strays found in the public, from abuse and neglect cases, from feral cat colonies and from local kill shelters. Add to that, in 2013 our local pound only saved a mere 18% of "healthy, adoptable" cats and kittens. The pressure that we face on a day-to-day basis is life versus death. If we don't step up to help, there are no "back-up's" to call on in our area.

But I digress...two days later we were elated to help a mom cat and her newborn kittens and we traveled to the address given to rescue them. We knocked on the door to the house several times prior to receiving an answer. The door creaked open as a large dog lunged toward us. The man was confused and the home was dark. I waited outside by the car, ready with food and water. Amy walked into the house letting the door close behind her as the dog stayed close at her heels watching her every move. The man retreated to an even darker basement and a moment later appeared with a sealed Tupperware container which he handed over. The mom and her newborn kittens were inside. Amy scurried out of the house as quickly as she could and as she approached the car, she threw open the lid to the box and we found that only one kitten remained alive. The box was full of steam as the mom cat had urinated and defecated while sealed in the box for two days. They all sat in the dampness of her excrement. The one newborn baby who had survived was barely hanging on. His eyes were not open yet and he was gasping for air; it had been too long. Meanwhile, the mom cat took in her first few breaths of fresh air in days. She was covered in the wetness of her own waste, terribly emaciated and dangerously dehydrated. We poured a fresh bowl of water and watched her lap up the smooth liquid with enthusiasm. Next we opened a can of wet cat food and she devoured the food with vigor. Afterwards she moved towards her only surviving kitten to bathe him and curled up in a ball amongst the nest of blankets we had created for her in her large pet crate. The gray and white mom cat couldn't have been more than a year old herself. We named her Libby and sadly her remaining baby did not survive the night. Libby was exhausted and defeated, although we knew she appreciated the constant love, affection, fresh food, water and veterinary care; her heart was broken.

After nearly two months of physical and emotional rehabilitation in her foster home, we were working on a project to save three death row shelter kittens. Libby's foster mom agreed to foster the kittens, along with Libby. Magically within moments of being introduced to each other, Libby began to mother the three orphaned kittens (new fosters). She bathed them, cuddled with them and watched over them and as she did this, her own broken heart began to heal.

The need for the rescue of companion animals is astounding. United States shelters currently kill more than 50% of adoptable cats and dogs annually; a number that can be drastically changed for the better as additional qualified rescue organizations are established and as competent, compassionate shelter directors are hired. In our own county, less than 18% of healthy, adoptable cats left the pound alive in 2013; while a mere 30% of healthy, adoptable dogs left the shelter doors alive. The rest left in body bags, as if they never existed or mattered. Those innocent pets who are left in body bags were owner surrendered pets (guardians who said they were moving, didn't have enough time for the pet, had a baby, had sudden allergies, et cetera), they were feral cats who could have lived out their lives on one of the many local farms after being altered, they were neglected and abused pets who hid in the back of their cramped cages afraid someone new might harm them. They were senior pets who the shelter saw as "unadoptable" and unwanted. They were special needs pets who may have looked a bit different but could have lived long, happy, healthy lives nonetheless. They were black cats and dogs who because of the color of their fur are quickly deemed "unadoptable" as they are so often not the first picks among adopters. They were living, breathing lives who just wanted a chance to survive, but due to one shelter director's daily decisions, they didn't get that chance. Their fate had been decided for them by those who turned them into the shelter; the decision to kill them being finalized by the shelter director.

We've worked with countless open intake shelters as they begin their journeys to become No Kill communities. It is possible to work together when a collaborative effort is established. In our own county, we worked for 11 years until we were finally given clearance to be the first approved rescue organization to work with the pound to pull *some* of the death row pets in need. It's a start, but a great deal more is needed. While in the shelter recently to save a batch of orphaned kittens, a terrified young mom cat and her two-week old kittens sat in one of the nearby cages. Our volunteer asked if we could pull them too. She explained that she had room to foster a new feline family in need now. The director said the mom cat was "feral" (although she appeared to simply be scared in the cramped, loud environment of the shelter). Our foster volunteer said that she didn't mind if the mom cat was scared and she was willing to work with her on socialization. In addition, she offered that if the mom did turn out to be feral, she lived on several acres of land and had heated cat huts and would allow the altered cat to live freely on her property once the babies were weaned. The shelter director shot her down instantly, fighting for what he saw as control and telling her "I'm not comfortable with that." Instead of letting the cat live, instead of letting the cat go to a foster home and eventually a forever home, he saw the death of a nursing mom cat as a better solution. A week later, we received a call that the two orphaned kittens needed rescue and to be bottle-fed. Their mom was no longer here to do the feeding (the shelter had killed her). So although we have made great strides in being "approved" to pull from the local pound, there is a lot more work to be done.

Pets in need are all ages, breeds and sizes. One day while at the shelter to save several cats in need, we came across two large adult cats huddled together in their small cage. We were told the cats were owner surrendered and no veterinary paperwork or records had been left, they hadn't even passed along their names. So there they sat, huddled together, holding each other in their dark cage, not knowing what would happen next. But we knew they were next in line to leave in a body bag that day. After making a few calls to our foster homes we were able to secure a foster home for the two of them together in our network and we successfully pulled the two adult cats to safety. They had been previously spayed/neutered and declawed and on the ride home they continued to hold each other, the female wrapping her arms around the back of the male.

Rescue is needed when it's done the right way. Over more than a decade of working in animal rescue, we've encountered both rescues and shelters who operate on the fly. That's when things quickly go south for the animals in need. All too often, those who start a rescue organization have big hearts but a lack of business sense. They want to save the animals, their intentions are positive, but the follow through is lacking. When you agree to take in an animal as a foster pet in your rescue, the animals must receive proper testing and veterinary care prior to entering the foster homes (more on this later). It is also important to verify that the foster homes' personal pets are up to date on vaccinations, healthy and spayed/neutered. Furthermore, the foster home needs to be the right match for the new foster pet. If you have a terribly shy or frightened pet and you place him in a lively foster home with children and other pets, issues are going to arise quickly. Operating an animal rescue isn't just about saving the animals, it's about providing proper veterinary care for every pet (first and foremost spay/neuter), proper food, water, shelter and adequate love, attention and rehabilitation training. In addition, how will you find qualified adopters for each of your pets? What will you do if you have an aggressive pet? Rescuing the pet is just the tip of the iceberg. What follows requires a strong business model, hard work and one of the most important aspects of running any business…great communication skills!

When individuals contact you for assistance, you should reply within 48 hours of their request and should always offer guidance. Operating an animal rescue organization is a 24/7 business; you don't get a break on holidays or birthdays. You will not be able to take in every pet that you are asked to help, but you can always offer other resources that may be able to provide a solution to help the animal in need. **Your words have the power to help, as much as your actions.**

When my own dog passed away from old age, I was devastated. Her name was Grandma and we rescued her from a shelter after she was deemed vicious and unadoptable. She was a senior dog at the time and in horrible health. She was a foster pet turned forever pet for me. She fit in great with my other two rescue dogs and we had three wonderful years together before she passed. At Advocates 4 Animals, our rescue focus is on cats. After a bit of time, I felt ready to save another senior dog in need and I began my search. I contacted shelters, pounds and rescue organizations alike in search of a senior dog who needed help. I wanted to provide a senior dog with a loving home, who would otherwise not have one. But my search only lead to endless frustration and for the first time I found myself on the opposite side of the adoption table. Instead of being the foster mom who helped potential adopters find the right match, I was now the potential adopter in search of assistance myself. Or rather, I should say I was in search of a reply! We contacted close to twenty area rescues, shelters and pounds and in the first week we only were able to actually speak with two. One was a kill shelter in Indiana who had four potential senior dogs needing help, but the individual we spoke with didn't know anything about them. The other was a dog focused rescue organization who was pleasantly responsive and helpful. As for the other 18 organizations, we were left without a reply. We called, left countless messages, wrote emails introducing ourselves and even filled out adoption applications…all were left without a reply. More than a month after the inquiries (and after we had found and adopted a special needs senior dog from the local dog rescue organization who had kindly responded the same week we contacted them) we received two more replies that were short and unhelpful. One said they wanted to know which dog we were interested in (even though it clearly stated the dog's name in our original email they were replying to) the other reply said that they would work on getting back to us. We never heard back from any of the others. It was a real wake-up call for what adopters are experiencing! It wasn't just from pounds or shelters, it was from rescue organizations too. The lack of response was disheartening. Our focus from the beginning at Advocates 4 Animals has always been on responsiveness and communication (and it is difficult when you are bombarded with hundreds of emails, texts and phone calls on a daily basis) but it is do-able if you make communication one of your priorities. It is a must for any successful business model. Without communication, you cannot find foster homes, adopters, donors, et cetera for your operation. Friendly, respectful and responsive communication is essential. Set specific hours during the work week and weekends which you will devote to e-mails, phone calls and other forms of communication and stick to it. As with any viable business, you will ride the roller-coaster of ups and downs. Be sure to realize that your top concerns are the welfare of the animals in your care and your daily communications with potential adopters, your foster homes, volunteers and potential donors.

At Advocates 4 Animals, it's always our goal to provide each potential adopter with a positive experience so that in the future, if they decide to add to their furry family, they will choose to adopt a rescue pet again. Whether it's from us or another rescue or shelter organization, our goal is to promote the adoption of rescue pets and to help each adopter have a memorable experience that they will then share with others. With some eight million rescue pets waiting for homes annually in our country alone, we need to do everything we can to promote adoption into loving, committed homes.

## CHAPTER 1- CHALLENGE:

- What are the euthanasia statistics at your local pound and/or shelter? What are their intake numbers and where are the majority of their intakes coming from (i.e. owner surrenders, senior pets, ill pets, etc.?) Is the shelter/pound an open-intake facility? Is their director willing to work with local 501(c)3 rescue organizations?

- How many 501(c)3 rescue organizations are in your area? Are they volunteer-based? Do they have facilities? What is each rescue organizations main focus (i.e. dogs under 10-pounds, a specific breed of dog, et cetera)?

- How many 501(c)3 organizations work to help feral cats in your area (through TNR methods)?

**Pawsitive**
**Connection**

*Heartwarming stories of*
*animals finding people*
*when we need them most*

Stacey Ritz

Volume I

# YOUR FREE SAMPLE CHAPTER OF *PAWSITIVE CONNECTION – VOLUME I*

# Forward

We save each other. I am grateful to experience the power of positive connection time and again throughout my life. I started rescuing stray and injured animals in need as soon as I could walk, so I suppose it has always been in my DNA to co-found an animal welfare organization to assist animals in need on a larger platform. As for my words- my parents recorded my first word as *"talks a lot!"* in my neatly kept baby book. They claim that once I started talking, I didn't stop. I guess some things never change. I channel that raw spirit and energy into my writing, in an effort to share my experiences with you.

Life teaches us many lessons over the course of our years. If we are lucky, we learn that life isn't about money or things; life is about connection to other living beings. My experience continues to teach me that we often surround ourselves with mirror images of our inner selves. When we feel scared, we may witness that same phenomenon in others. When we are ready to move forward and heal from persisting deep wounds, we align ourselves with those who will support our transformation. When we're uncertain about the trajectory of our life, we see that same fear in those around us. So often it is our companion animals who find us when we are most in need. From my own ongoing adventures in animal rescue to the heartwarming stories that have been shared with me by others, I am absolutely certain that the human-animal bond has the power to heal, transform and enlighten each of our lives.

This book is a collection of true stories of *Pawsitive Connection* between pets (both cats and dogs) and humans, written from my own observations and opinions. It is my hope that the stories will resonate with each of you, as in the end, we are all connected. Animals have a mystical way of finding us when we need them most, even if we don't know it yet. But it is up to us to be alert and accepting of their healing powers; and when we are miracles truly can occur.

# Chapter 1: The Power of Connection

*"Blessed in the person who has earned the love of an old dog." –Sydney Jeanne Seward*

The first night of her passing, I desperately wished that I had a favorite toy or blanket to hold onto. We rescued her in 2011 after she had been callously dumped at a kill-shelter and deemed "vicious" (and therefore unadoptable). She was living in fear. Her feet had never known a ground other than rusty wire cages. She was heavily infested with fleas (to the point of having lost all of her fur). She had burn marks on her back end- guessed to be a type of torture method used in cruel breeding practices. The emaciated tan and white Chihuahua weighed just 5 lbs. and her eyes were dim and hopeless. She wouldn't allow shelter volunteers near her- she would growl and lunge towards them, terrified for her life. Her nipples hung low from more than a decade of constant breeding. She was significantly underweight and dehydrated. Most of all, she was terrified.

I primarily fostered cats, but when the shelter volunteer reached out and sent me the photo of the elderly, terrified Chihuahua (who desperately needed rescue along with her suspected daughter, dumped at the shelter with her) my intuition told me I needed to save them, to foster them- to *give them a chance.* I was never a "small dog person" having shared my home in the past with large breed dogs such as Rottweiler mixes and the like. **But there is a powerful force at play when you listen to your gut.** And in this instance (I am so grateful) I listened to mine.

*We named her Grandma*, as she was estimated to be 12-15 years old at the time of rescue. Her daughter was estimated to be around 5 years old and after she was given the medical care she needed, spayed and fully vetted she was adopted to an incredibly loving home where she was given the name Charlotte.

Grandma, on the other hand, had several serious issues; life-threatening issues. Grandma's teeth were each hanging by a thread- some of them hanging by less than that. Her gums were filled with pus and she was in significant pain. She needed dental surgery and all but 3 teeth were removed immediately. She also needed to be spayed. The day she was spayed, our veterinarian called us to let us know if the spay had taken place even one day later, Grandma would have died. But we had the surgery done just in time. No one knew, but when they opened Grandma up for her spay surgery, it was discovered that she had pyometra- which most likely was caused by being bred in filthy conditions for more than a decade of life. Grandma miraculously survived and made a full recovery from her surgeries, all the while, we grew a strong bond. She ran in the grass for the first time, played with other dogs for the first time- and I mean really played! She flipped her toys in the air and growled with feistiness, as if she were a young puppy just discovering life. Grandma, having lived her entire life in a crate, was not potty trained. But she followed the lead of my two resident dogs and caught on fairly quickly. Her eyes had a light that communicated her immense happiness to be alive and to be here.

Knowing her story, her age and her struggles with life-saving surgeries- and the strength of our bond that only continued to grow- we decided to officially adopt her (as if there were ever any question!). She fit like a glove. She got along great with our other two dogs and slept next to me in bed every night. She came to work with me, she went for car rides, we went on daily walks, lots of hikes in the woods and she had all of the spunk and energy of a young adult. Her hair grew in, and in time she reached a healthy, ideal weight of 9 lbs. Her burn marks went away and her happiness was palpable. She attached herself to me and I smiled and laughed more than I had in years.

In my personal life, I had suffered a debilitating sexual assault in 2008 and had been unable to cope with the ramifications surrounding the incident. I refused to speak about it and struggled to move forward. But when Grandma entered my life, things began to change. Grandma always wanted to be with me, sitting on my lap, snuggling, going for walks- you name it. She was right there by my side. And never in my life had I felt the loyalty of another living being in this strength. I had wonderful people in my life and I had shared my home with many special animals over the years, but there was something different about Grandma. Despite all that I had endured in my personal life, I knew Grandma would not abandon me emotionally. I knew I could just be me and I was accepted. There was something huge in that realization- and it was the start of my journey of emotional transformation.

**Everything in our lives, everything that surrounds us is a mirror of ourselves.** Realizing this now I am in awe at the gravity of its truth. And as for the Grandma and me, we healed each other.

We had three wonderful years. **I find myself wishing for one more day, one more walk, one more ride in the car...but I know that would only leave me wishing for another.** I miss her dearly and I feel lost without her. The month before she passed I began to feel a transformation in myself. I began to feel healed from the past trauma. I was able to let it go and move forward. I was living again. I was laughing again. My relationships had grown stronger and I had learned to trust- a gift I never expected would come.

Looking back, I realize the many lessons Grandma taught me- and continues to teach me even in her absence. She taught me that it's okay to be an adult and play- in fact it makes life so much more fun! She taught me that connection is real. She taught me that our eyes truly are the gateway to the soul. Grandma taught me that it's important to really listen when someone you love is talking to you, and she taught me that it's okay to look silly when you're excited. *The important thing is to be excited each and every time you see the ones you love*- never feel embarrassed to express your love- because you never know how many of those moments you'll have. She taught me that if you make known what you want in life (persistence!) that you will inevitably get it. She taught me to laugh. She taught me to never give up hope because you never know what might be around the next bend. She taught me that connection is what makes life worth living. She taught me to not be afraid of showing my teeth (it's okay to growl if something- or someone- bothers you); *speak up!* She taught me the meaning of unconditional love. And perhaps most of all, Grandma taught me to put the ones you connect with in life first. **If you have someone who loves you and you love them back you are incredibly lucky and blessed.**

As Grandma made a full recovery of her own and thrived, I began following her lead. Many times, talking about her in conversations served as an ice-breaker (given her unique name and her story). She went on beach vacations and even spent time in New York City with me walking through the hustle and bustle of it all. We were there for each other through our transformations.

Every day of her life, since rescue, was filled with happiness, laughter and love. During her final week she continued to have the same spunk she's carried with her since rescue; but at night she would insist on sleeping pressed tightly against me, her head on my pillow. My intuition told me her time was nearing and I tried my best to stay up for as long as I could each night giving her belly rubs and telling her how much I loved her. The day she passed, her breathing had quickly become strained. Her heart was giving out from old age. Her eyes told me she was ready for my help and we called our veterinarian. I held her in a blanket on my lap and before we left our street, from my lap, cradled in my arms, Grandma glanced up at me one last time and then quickly buried her head in the crook of my arm as I felt her leave. And just like that, she was gone.

Now I find myself wishing I had a favorite toy or blanket of hers to treasure. But then I was reminded that she didn't have a favorite of those things because I was her favorite thing. And what more could I ask for? *Knowing this was perhaps one of the greatest gifts she gave me.*

I believe that often animals find us at the right times. We may not recognize it in the moment, but something else is at play. Two days after Grandma's passing, still a wreck in her absence, I received a message to call my own Grandma (my human Grandma). It sounded urgent. I did my best to muster up the strength to talk through my own pain (and lots of tears) – and made the call to my Grandma. While not divulging the conversation in its totality, the talk we had that night was the most personal, meaningful conversation we had ever had. She told me that she (not knowing about Grandma's passing) had an overwhelming urge to speak with me this week. I was humbled by her words and a special promise she asked me to make to her during that phone call. Throughout the conversation she repeatedly thanked me for calling her and told me how happy it made her to feel near me. It's a feeling and a conversation I will never forget.

When I woke up the next morning the Native American saying, *"There are more things unseen and unknown than known and seen"* played on repeat in my head.

As published in Advocates 4 Animals Blog – August 2014

# A Few of the things Grandma taught me:

- It's okay to be goofy with the ones you love. Who cares what you look like? Happiness and laughter are what life is all about!

- It doesn't matter how old or young you are- when you have the opportunity to run through the grass with your bare feet, do it with wild abandon.

- Never stop being curious. Adventure can always be found when your eyes are open.

- It's okay to growl when you're upset. It's healthy to show your true emotions.

- When you see someone you love, show your excitement (don't hold back)!

- It's okay to ask for help. When you're too tired to keep going, ask for help and it will come.

- Don't hide yourself away. Be proud of who you are. When you are your authentic self you will undoubtedly make others smile.

- Always sleep in the position that is most comfortable. No questions asked.

- It's okay to bury your head under the covers when you don't want to get up in the morning. Sometimes a few more minutes of quiet can go a long way.

- Barking is good! If something doesn't seem right, speak up.

- Enjoy the sunshine. Get outside daily and bask in the light- you'll be glad you did.

- Never underestimate the power of love and loyalty.

# DON'T DELAY...
# PURCHASE TODAY!
## Available on Amazon in paperback and e-book formats

Made in the USA
San Bernardino, CA
13 March 2015